A Daily Dose

A Seed Devotional For Winners

By
PATRICE BRANTLEY

Copyright © 2019 by Live To Produce Publishing Group
A Daily Dose: *A Seed Devotional For Winners*
By Patrice Brantley

Connect with us:
Facebook Group:
The Seed Sowing Sistah Movement
Email:
Theseedsowingsistahmovement@gmail.com
Printed in the United States of America.
All rights reserved under International Copyright Law. Contents and/or cover may not be reproduced in whole or part in any form without the express written consent of the writer.

ISBN: 978-0-9968628-9-9

Live To Produce
Publishing Group
Mesa, AZ 85212

WHAT OTHERS ARE SAYING ABOUT PATRICE AND THE DAILY DOSE FROM THE SEED SOWING SISTAH

The Morning Seed you have sent to me for nearly a year now feels like my own personal daily devotion. The readings and questions to ponder can help keep things in perspective for me and to remember God's promises and words especially during time of despair, sadness, anger, frustration, joy, humility, and the like. I look forward to reading them when I wake up and sometimes I re- read throughout the day to keep myself in the present of here and now.

Leslie

The Morning Seed has impacted my life with "Encouragement!"

Sherry

Hi Brantley, both you and the Morning Seed have made a huge impact on my life in your teaching, prayers [of] encouragement and uplifting inspirational messages. You have motivated me to grow closer to God and seek his purpose for my life. For this I'm very grateful and say thank you from the bottom of my heart and pray that God will continue working thru you to help many more.

Eurina

Dear Peace purpose, I would like to say that your daily prayer messages has kept me focused on the Bible verse and your examples about it close to me in a positive way. It takes me from my daily routines to a time well spent in reflection of our Lord's promises. I thank you and will continue to pray for your love of the Lord and his word and may it never leave you.

Your sister in Christ,

Florance

Patrice is doing what most people dream of, as she is invested and in love with the Lord. Unlike most, Patrice uses every opportunity, to not reflect upon herself, or her word-but seeks to reflect the Lord and His work and His Word all while going about her journey. Patrice, you have touched my heart and so many others. Your mission brings DAILY energy and life to the greatest story ever told. May our good and merciful Lord favor you and be merciful to you all your days.

A. Powell 🙏

Ms. Brantley and "The Morning Seed" has really helped me understand some of the stories in the Bible...I love it! Yes, I set time aside to read "The Seed," and I challenge EVERYONE that receives it in the morning to put aside 5 to 10 minutes to read it. We read and listen to everything else...why not listen to GOD's word for a moment! Thanks for all that you do sis! It is NOT DONE IN VAIN! Much love.

Tammy 🙈🙏❤️

The morning seed is a connection to remain focused in line upon line and precept upon precept. Christ is real daily! Therefore, daily we need to be informed to stay on track in Christ.

J. Grice

It's always pleasant, to have a good word, for starting the day, or even to go back to it sometime during the day.

Avia

Special Acknowledgements

This book was birth through a simple prayer where I asked the LORD to help me be creativity and encourage others.... Well little did I know that he would answer that prayer in this way. Enjoy my passion and purpose, his power, and the HOLY SPIRIT's presence.

Dedication

This book is dedicated to my late and great girlfriend Lenora P. who saw the GREATNESS in me when I couldn't see it in myself. Your laughter, life, and love will forever live in my heart.

This book is also dedicated to my sistah circle who cheered, encouraged, ignited a fire under me with love, and prayed with me and for me in all seasons of my life. You all are my cheerleaders and I love you all to life and to the moon and back.

A SEED DEVOTIONAL FOR WINNERS

DAILY DOSE

Happy New Beginning

A SEED DEVOTIONAL FOR WINNERS

Good Morning and Happy New Beginnings!!!

May this new beginning greet you with many marvelous blessings for you, your family, and friends. May this year approach you with barrels of bountiful blessings, carloads of compassion and cash, divine direction, heavenly health and heavenly assistance from the HOLY Spirit, and the discipline to explore and exalt the faithfulness and favor of your Glorious GOD, in order to become an individuals who doesn't just talk Jesus but carries his presence daily. May this year find you living in the moment to display the LORD's life and love as well as staying in a Kingdom Mindset and motivated state to Never give up on the challenges that lie ahead in your journey. May you openly accept every Opportunity for Greatness and have the Power to stay positive and prayerful. Using our mouths to bring a powerful praise of GOD's goodness where we experience GOD's Quality and Quantity in all areas of our lives. Receive this blessing and pour out a powerful praise to get your day and New Year started.

Have a splendid day.

A SEED DEVOTIONAL FOR WINNERS

A SEED DEVOTIONAL FOR WINNERS

DAILY DOSE

Newness 2

A SEED DEVOTIONAL FOR WINNERS

Good Morning Amazing Children of GOD,

It all starts with the mind. Do you know what's the difference between an okay boxer and a world renowned champion boxer? Not the skills or the amount of training time. It all starts in the mind. When the late, great Muhammad Ali would prepare for a match he was very strategic about how he dealt with his opponents. He would get into his opponent's mind and tell them how they were going down and in what round. So let's look at this in the spiritual realm. In I Samuel 17 we see David standing strong and ready to destroy Goliath. The one thing that I love about this story is that David had a made up mind about who he represented and how the fight would be won. He just boasted on the LORD and stood sure footed about his upcoming victory.

Devine Decree: *My mind is made up and I am going all the way with the LORD. I know that if I have a made up mind at all times that he will NEVER fail ME!!!!*

Have a magnificent day.

A SEED DEVOTIONAL FOR WINNERS

A SEED DEVOTIONAL FOR WINNERS

DAILY DOSE

Newness 3

A SEED DEVOTIONAL FOR WINNERS

Good Morning Brilliant and Bold Children of GOD,

Pulling off your old self. Have you ever seen the picture of a person stepping out of their body or pulling off a mask. This is a clear example of pulling off the old man that the Bible speaks about in Ephesians 4:22-24. The old man symbolizes our corrupted and deceitful desires (our flesh). We are to be made new in our attitudes and mind.

Question to Ponder: *What are some of the old attitudes, behaviors or reactions that your old man needs to pull off?*

Divine Decree: *I am a new man who has been creatively crafted by God. Have an amazing day.*

A SEED DEVOTIONAL FOR WINNERS

A SEED DEVOTIONAL FOR WINNERS

DAILY DOSE

Confession Time

A SEED DEVOTIONAL FOR WINNERS

Good Morning Brilliant and Bold Children of GOD,

Confession time: After several years of being in a very abusive and hostile work environment, I was finally relocated to my new location and position. To my surprise, when I got to the new location and position I experienced some of the same behaviors in the management team as the former. I instantly started having some of the same old attitudes, and was quickly checked by the Holy Spirit about how I was handling this new place. The HOLY Spirit showed me two things.

1. *The first thing that was revealed to me was that I had been elevated to another level, and things had changed for the better, but this place will still have its challenges.*

2. *The second thing revealed to me was that I had moved to another location and position, but my attitude didn't change. Talk about a hard pill to swallow. However, as time went on my attitude changed for the better. The lesson learned was you can't represent GOD, The HOLY Spirt, and Jesus with an unchanged mind and funky attitude.*

A SEED DEVOTIONAL FOR WINNERS

So today's verses to mediate on are Ephesians 4:22-24 (NIV) "You were taught, with regard to your former way of life, to put off your old self, which is being corrupted by its deceitful desires; to be made new in the attitude of your minds; and to put on the new self, created to be like God in true righteousness and holiness."

Question to ponder: Have I truly stepped into the New Year with a New Mindset and Attitude?

Have a wonderful day.

A SEED DEVOTIONAL FOR WINNERS

A SEED DEVOTIONAL FOR WINNERS

DAILY DOSE

Newness 4

A SEED DEVOTIONAL FOR WINNERS

Good Morning Cheerleaders of a Glorious GOD,

A new heart and a new spirit Bible verses for today: Acts chapters 7,8,9 and Ezekiel 18:30-32 (NIV)

Have you ever seen or heard a heart that has been damaged? Sure you have because when the person speaks you hear the pain of the wound oozing out. Have you ever heard a dirty/toxic spirit? Yes, because the person seems to be easily swayed with the popular opinion in order to avoid the stings and bruises of other people's opinions or nothing but negative spews out. In the story of Saul transforming to PAUL we see both sides; in Acts chapter 7 & 8, his heart was once toxic and full of hate for the LORD and his faithful Christians and that his spirit was so intertwined in the hate that he was murdering Christians. See Acts Chapters 7 & 8.

However, in chapter 9 Saul had an amazing encounter with the LORD on the way to Damascus where the LORD opened Saul's EYES in the SPIRIT and cleaned up his HEART all at the SAME time!!! The one touch from the LORD not only made him a ROCKSTAR in the Kingdom of Heaven for preaching and teaching the gospel, it also made him an advocate for others in the Christian world. Can you truly imagine a man who once was on a war path for Satan being turned around and being a true Gospel Gangster Legend for the HEAVENLY Kingdom? If one touch did that for Saul,

A SEED DEVOTIONAL FOR WINNERS

can you truly imagine what it can do for YOU when you have a clean heart and spirit?

Power Prayer: LORD touch me with the same power and compassion that you touched Saul with. LORD I eagerly await your touch to my heart and my spirit. Clean up the areas in my heart, life, and spirit that doesn't reflect you.

Have a HOLY Spirit spiritually touched day.

A SEED DEVOTIONAL FOR WINNERS

A SEED DEVOTIONAL FOR WINNERS

DAILY DOSE

New Attire

A SEED DEVOTIONAL FOR WINNERS

Good Morning Devine Decreers,

One of my favorite parts of my current job is seeing the transformation of the people I work with. It reminds me so much of the 1st day of school because they are now fully dressed for success not just on the outside, but on the inside. This sometimes takes three months or more depending on the level of their change.

Question to Ponder: *What are some of the transformations you are making to glorify God in your life?*

Divine Decree: *I am a heavenly caterpillar beautifully and bountifully transforming into the butterfly that God has made me.*

Have an amazing day.

A SEED DEVOTIONAL FOR WINNERS

A SEED DEVOTIONAL FOR WINNERS

DAILY DOSE

Rahab: The Unlikely Choice

A SEED DEVOTIONAL FOR WINNERS

Good Morning Lively Children of Christ, Bible Connection: Joshua Chapter 2

I remember as a kid not being picked for any of the teams when it came to kickball. This went on for years because I was the husky girl with coke bottle glasses who HATED to run. The only time I ran back then was for the ice cream truck... 😂😂😂 Yet, I never really got over the hurt of not being chosen by my classmates. So I remember having a tearful conversation with my Grandmother about this. I can still hear her words so clear, "When man rejects you know that GOD has selected you." This one statement has helped me through some pretty tough times and dealing with unwanted rejection from others. Let's look at a Mighty Woman of GOD in the Bible who was rejected by man because of her profession, but selected by GOD in his prefect plan of selection. In Joshua Chapter 2 we meet a PROSTITUTE named Rahab who helped two Israelites soldiers spy out the land of their GODLY inheritance. She was wise in how she honored the men of GOD and in how she helped them to escape the pure danger of the KING's search party.

A SEED DEVOTIONAL FOR WINNERS

So, where men saw a Prostitute. GOD saw a willing and obedient heart ready to obey his instructions.

Question to ponder: Think about it when GOD sends someone to you. Are you busy looking on the outside and perhaps missing the BLESSING on the inside?

Have an amazing day!!!

A SEED DEVOTIONAL FOR WINNERS

A SEED DEVOTIONAL FOR WINNERS

DAILY DOSE

Perceiving The GODLY Presence

A SEED DEVOTIONAL FOR WINNERS

Good Morning Powerful People of Insight,

Did you know that there is a difference between a man and a true GODLY man? The GODLY man has a presence that shows all the fruit of the spirit where an average man has none. The fruits of the spirit are love, joy, peace, patience, kindness, goodness, faithfulness, gentleness and self-control. In the story of Rahab these fruits were shown in such a way that she couldn't mistake these men for anything else but True men of GOD. So let's flip the mirror.

When you present yourself to the world are you displaying the fruits of the spirit or fruits of the flesh? Just something to think about.

Scripture Connection: Joshua 2: 8-14 (NIV) "Before the spies lay down for the night, she went up on the roof and said to them, 'I know that the LORD has given you this land and that a great fear of you has fallen on us, so that all who live in this country are melting in fear because of you. We have heard how the LORD dried up the water of the Red Sea for you when you came out of Egypt, and what you did to Sihon and Og, the two kings of the Amorites east of the Jordan, whom you completely destroyed.

A SEED DEVOTIONAL FOR WINNERS

When we heard of it, our hearts melted in fear and everyone's courage failed because of you, for the LORD your God is God in heaven above and on the earth below. "Now then, please swear to me by the LORD that you will show kindness to my family, because I have shown kindness to you.

Give me a sure sign" "Now then, please swear to me by the LORD that you will show kindness to my family, because I have shown kindness to you.

Give me a sure sign that you will spare the lives of my father and mother, my brothers and sisters, and all who belong to them—and that you will save us from death.' 'Our lives for your lives!' the men assured her. 'If you don't tell what we are doing, we will treat you kindly and faithfully when the LORD gives us the land.'

Have an insightful day.

A SEED DEVOTIONAL FOR WINNERS

A SEED DEVOTIONAL FOR WINNERS

DAILY DOSE

Who Are You Servicing

A SEED DEVOTIONAL FOR WINNERS

Good Morning Soulful Servants of GOD,

In the story Rahab we see her being a servant in two realms. In the (Worldly) natural world she was servicing sex and shelter for the men who stopped by for a good time. Yet, in the spiritual realm she was servicing a willing and obedient heart up to GOD through food, shelter, and safety for the men of GOD.

Question to ponder: So the question for today is WHO and WHAT are you servicing?

Divine Decree: I am a heavenly made problem solver, God has created me to solve problems with heavenly assistance.

Have a simply beautiful day.

A SEED DEVOTIONAL FOR WINNERS

A SEED DEVOTIONAL FOR WINNERS

DAILY DOSE

Protected By God's Hand

A SEED DEVOTIONAL FOR WINNERS

Good Morning Powerfully Protected Children of GOD, Bible Scripture: Joshua 2:4-10

Have you ever seen a first time mother? She can spend hours looking at her precious newborn. She uses the utmost care to bathe, clean, dress, and feed her new baby. She will also take the time to teach her baby about the world's dangers, and if it is truly dangerous she will lay down her life for her baby. This is the same way GOD used Rahab. In Joshua chapter 2 Rahab instructed the two soldiers to go up into the hill country where they would be safe, and told the king's men to search the roads about the city. This one act showed her fierce mothering side to protect the soldiers and ultimately ended up protecting the promise of saving herself and her family from the impending deaths when Joshua and his men were to possess the city.

Question to ponder: Can you think of a time when the hand of GOD's protected/saved you from yourself or from someone else?

Have a wonderful day

A SEED DEVOTIONAL FOR WINNERS

A SEED DEVOTIONAL FOR WINNERS

DAILY DOSE

Crossing Over Your Jordan: God's Time

A SEED DEVOTIONAL FOR WINNERS

Good Morning Christ Carriers, Bible Scriptures: Joshua chapter 3

Have you ever been trying to make moves in life, and they don't work out? I remember trying to leave the school system for a few years. I would go on interviews and would sometimes get the job only to end up turning the job down due to an unforeseen circumstance. Yet, when it was time to finally move into my NEWNESS all stumbling blocks had been removed and I was free to move on. I am sharing this so we don't get frustrated and give up on the promise that GOD has shown or spoken to you.

****Remember that GOD's timing is truly Devine Timing.****

Question to ponder: Are you running behind God, ahead of God, or with God?

Have a wonderful day.

A SEED DEVOTIONAL FOR WINNERS

A SEED DEVOTIONAL FOR WINNERS

DAILY DOSE

Crossing Over Your Jordan: God's Rest

A SEED DEVOTIONAL FOR WINNERS

Good Morning Well Rested Followers of Jesus Christ,

Bible Scriptures: Joshua chapter 3

Have you ever had to take a long journey by car? Once you get the car packed and have prepared several snacks for the journey, how do you rest for the upcoming journey? Well, when you are going on a trip and GOD is your guide he will give you HIS SWEET REST. Today remember that GOD's rest is the best rest.

Questions to ponder: Am I resting in God before preparing to go on this new journey? Am I mentally prepared for the journey that God has me on?

Have a wonderful day.

A SEED DEVOTIONAL FOR WINNERS

A SEED DEVOTIONAL FOR WINNERS

DAILY DOSE

Crossing Over Your Jordan: God's Instruction

A SEED DEVOTIONAL FOR WINNERS

Good Morning Well Ignited 🔥 Children of GOD,

Do you remember when you were in Elementary School and the teacher would give you instructions? Well think about the different types of students. Student A would hear the instructions and start working immediately.

Student B would hear the instructions and delay starting. Student C would be in their own world and the teacher would have to repeat the instructions.

Now I have to admit that I have been ALL of these students...probably more like Student C until the belt got involved then I moved straight up to Student A (Mae don't play no games with the belt). So let's look at this in the spiritual realm. When GOD gives you instructions which student are you? Truly think about it. In the story of Joshua and the Israelites they heeded the instructions and moved quickly.

Special Side Note: When you heed the instructions you are to move WITH GOD. Not ahead or behind unless he has instructed you like the children of Israel.

Bible Scriptures: Joshua 3:3-4 (NIV) "giving orders to the people:

A SEED DEVOTIONAL FOR WINNERS

'When you see the ark of the covenant of the LORD your God, and the Levitical priests carrying it, you are to move out from your positions and follow it. Then you will know which way to go, since you have never been this way before. But keep a distance of about two thousand cubits between you and the ark; do not go near it.'

Have a wonderful day.

A SEED DEVOTIONAL FOR WINNERS

A SEED DEVOTIONAL FOR WINNERS

DAILY DOSE

Crossing Over Your Jordan: God's Instruction Pt 2.

A SEED DEVOTIONAL FOR WINNERS

Good Morning Well Focused People of GOD,

Bible Scriptures: Joshua 3:5 (NIV) "Joshua told the people, 'Consecrate yourselves, for tomorrow the LORD will do amazing things among you."

So let's go back to that Elementary Classroom with the students. Remember when your teacher would give you two step directions? The teacher would break the directions into two parts. Direction part 1 and Direction part 2. For example, students put your Math books away and line up at the back door. Many times GOD does US the same way to see if you are going to clearly follow direction number 1 before he gives you direction number 2. In this case direction number 2 was to "Consecrate yourselves." When you consecrate yourself, you are setting yourself apart from sin and repenting from any past sin and not going back to those same sins.

Side note: When you complete both sets of directions you are moving closer to truly Crossing into YOUR Jordan.

Have a wonderful day.

A SEED DEVOTIONAL FOR WINNERS

A SEED DEVOTIONAL FOR WINNERS

DAILY DOSE

Crossing Over Your Jordan: The Elevation

A SEED DEVOTIONAL FOR WINNERS

Good Morning Heavenly Elevated Children of God,

Think back to the 1st time you were put in charge in the house. You were the kid in charge while mom or dad was gone. You got to control the TV; answer the phone, if you were allowed to; and tell your younger siblings what to do. And, guess what, you had your parent or parents backing you up on your decisions. This is the same way GOD wants to elevate you in the Heavenly Kingdom. He wants to be able to leave you to make GODLY decisions that he can stand back with you and say well done my child. I knew you could do it!!! Also remember that Man's elevations comes with strings, while GOD's elevation comes with WINGS

Bible Scriptures: Joshua 3:5-7 (NIV) "Joshua told the people, 'Consecrate yourselves, for tomorrow the LORD will do amazing things among you.' Joshua said to the priests, 'Take up the ark of the covenant and pass on ahead of the people.' So they took it up and went ahead of them. And the LORD said to Joshua, 'Today I will begin to exalt you in the eyes of all Israel, so they may know that I am with you as I was with Moses.'

Have a wonderful day.

A SEED DEVOTIONAL FOR WINNERS

A SEED DEVOTIONAL FOR WINNERS

DAILY DOSE

Crossing Over Your Jordan: The Water The Final Chapter

A SEED DEVOTIONAL FOR WINNERS

Good Morning World Class Water Walkers,

Have you ever noticed that right before your BREAKTHROUGH you are under so much attack and it feels like a tidal wave is coming for you and you are not sure which way to turn? Well just imagine how the children of Israel felt when they were once again between a rock and a watery place. I can hear them talking now, "What do we do now? How will GOD bring us out of this?" Just as the Levites' and priests' toes touched to the edge of the Jordan River it stopped flowing and lined up as a wall, and all the Israelites were able to cross on dry land. Let's look at this in your life realm. When it seems like there is nowhere to turn and no way out. GOD shows up and shows ALL the WAY OUT in a way that you can't help but give him praise for your Water experience that ultimately lead to your Breakthrough that ushered you into your Bountifully Blessed Life!! (Psss...If you are not sure that was your part to shout)

Testimony time: Share a quick testimony about your life. Have a Beautifully Blessed day.

A SEED DEVOTIONAL FOR WINNERS

A SEED DEVOTIONAL FOR WINNERS

DAILY DOSE

Your Purification Process: The Messenger And The Message

A SEED DEVOTIONAL FOR WINNERS

Good Morning Passionate Prayer Partners,

Bible Scriptures: 2nd Kings 5:14

Dream Connection: About a week of more ago I had a dream that there was a huge abscess on my stomach. In the dream I popped it and pus flowed out like river. After a brief freak out I called my mom and told her the dream.

She explained that the dream was about the spirit being purified. So this is what inspired the theme for this week. In 2nd Kings 5:1-14 Naaman, a top Military commander has the disease of Leprosy. His young Israelite slave girl says to his wife that he needs to go to the PROPHET in Samaria to be healed. Naaman, being the smart man that he is, immediately hears and heeds the instructions.

Question to Ponder: When you are given a message. Do YOU hear and heed the message? Or Focus on the messenger? Think about it??

Have a marvelous day.

A SEED DEVOTIONAL FOR WINNERS

A SEED DEVOTIONAL FOR WINNERS

DAILY DOSE

Your Purification Process Pt.2
Your Support System

A SEED DEVOTIONAL FOR WINNERS

Good Morning Purposeful Praisers of GOD,

Bible Scriptures: 2nd Kings 5:1-14

"Lean on me, when you're not strong/ And I'll be your friend/ I'll help you carry on" (partial lyrics from Lean on Me by Bill Withers). Do you have a support system in your life? I am pretty sure the answer is yes. Who is a part of your support system? Maybe friends, family, church members or even a stranger. When you are going through your purification process you will need a truly prayerful support system. In 2nd Kings 5:4-6 Naaman's support system was his wife, servants, the slave girl and his boss (the King). Note: Having a support system doesn't make you weak it makes you whole.

Have a wonderful day.

A SEED DEVOTIONAL FOR WINNERS

A SEED DEVOTIONAL FOR WINNERS

DAILY DOSE

Your Purification Process Pt.3
Your Perspective

A SEED DEVOTIONAL FOR WINNERS

Good Morning Saints,

Bible Scriptures: 2nd Kings 5:7 (NIV) "As soon as the king of Israel read the letter, he tore his robes and said, 'Am I God? Can I kill and bring back to life? Why does this fellow send someone to me to be cured of his leprosy? See how he is trying to pick a quarrel with me!'

Dream Connection: Going back to the dream from the previous lesson about the abscess. When I first interpreted the dream I focused on the infection.

However, when my mother interpreted the same dream she saw a spiritual cleansing. Just like in the story the King of Israel and I had the wrong perspective and freaked out on something that I nor he had any power over. Today before you freak out over something check your perspective. You maybe freaking out over something that GOD has said was GOOD, but seeing it in the wrong LIGHT. #Checkyourperspective

Question to ponder: In your current situation, do you have a fleshly or spiritual perspective?

Have a wonderful day

A SEED DEVOTIONAL FOR WINNERS

A SEED DEVOTIONAL FOR WINNERS

DAILY DOSE

Your Purification Process Pt.4
Godly Resources

A SEED DEVOTIONAL FOR WINNERS

Good Morning Kingdom Carriers,

Bible Scriptures: 2nd Kings chapter 5

Do you know your GODLY Resources? What does a GODLY resources bring to you? In the story of Naaman, his GODLY resources were the Israelite slave girl, his wife, his boss (the King), and Prophet Elisha. Each of them brought him something towards his healing and wholeness. The Israel slave girl brought directions for his healing and the location of the Prophet (Elisha), his wife brought him the message and encouragement, the king gave him support and allowed him to travel, and Prophet Elisha allowed GOD to flow through him, guide him, and be an instrument of his complete healing and wholeness. This is shown by the instructions and the blessing of peace that he gives Naaman when he leaves. So today take time to discover who are your GODLY resources. If you are having trouble ask GOD, he will gladly lead you to them.

Power Prayer: Lord show me who are my Godly resources are and how to properly interact with them. Let me host them as if I am hosting you and the heavenly angels.

Have a HOLY Spirit led day.

A SEED DEVOTIONAL FOR WINNERS

A SEED DEVOTIONAL FOR WINNERS

DAILY DOSE

Your Purification Process Pt.5 No Titles Please

A SEED DEVOTIONAL FOR WINNERS

Good Morning Heavenly Helpers,

Bible Scriptures: 2nd Kings 5:9-11 (NIV) "So Naaman went with his horses and chariots and stopped at the door of Elisha's house. Elisha sent a messenger to say to him, 'Go, wash yourself seven times in the Jordan, and your flesh will be restored and you will be cleansed.' But Naaman went away angry and said, 'I thought that he would surely come out to me and stand and call on the name of the LORD his God, wave his hand over the spot and cure me of my leprosy.'

Have you ever met someone who constantly name dropped or found a way to drop their title or position in EVERY conversation? In Naaman's story he tried to impress the Prophet of GOD with his Earthly Title and position only to be quickly dismissed and directed to the Jordan River by one of the house servants. He thought that his earthly title would move a GODLY man. Sorry boo-boo earthly titles only move some earthly folks, but definitely not a REAL MAN or WOMAN of GOD.

Yo' titles don't move me. I work in and on a HEAVENLY System. #Whoyouboo? #2Kings 5:9-11

Have a HOLY Spirit led day.

A SEED DEVOTIONAL FOR WINNERS

A SEED DEVOTIONAL FOR WINNERS

DAILY DOSE

Purified, But Are You Picking Up Someone Else's Mess

A SEED DEVOTIONAL FOR WINNERS

Good Morning Amazing Children of GOD, Bible Scriptures: 2nd Kings 5:15-26

Have you ever had a good intention go horribly wrong? Well this week we will explore the dangers of good intentions. At the end of Naaman's healing we see that he is grateful and has a repentant heart. Yet, we also meet Gehazi the prophet's servant. He had in his heart to do something wonderful for the prophet but ultimately made a ME, MY, and I decision. His mouth said for the prophet, but in his heart he said for me. Today be careful not to let a good intention turn into a selfish decision.

Question to ponder: What are your true motives? Are they for peoples praise or for God's purpose.

Divine Decree: Lord create in me a clean and pure heart so that I can openly and willingly serve you.

Have a GODLY led day.

A SEED DEVOTIONAL FOR WINNERS

A SEED DEVOTIONAL FOR WINNERS

DAILY DOSE

Purified, But Running After Trouble

A SEED DEVOTIONAL FOR WINNERS

Good Morning Power Packed Children of GOD, Bible Scriptures: 2nd Kings 5:20-21

Have you ever had a moment in life where GOD said "NO" but you went running after the person or thing anyway? (Please don't let me be the only one with my hand raised!) In the story of Gehazi he took off running behind Naaman's chariot on the quest to do something great for the Prophet Elisha, yet when the chariot stopped the lies started and the web of deception began. Today, make a decision to leave any and all trouble behind and run TOWARDS what GOD is calling you TO DO.

Question to ponder: Am I running after earthly gain and in the process losing my soul?

Devine Decree: God I am only chasing after you and your will.

Have a wonderful day. 😁

#Ionlyrunforsoulfoodnow #runningforastrawberryshortcakewasmythang

A SEED DEVOTIONAL FOR WINNERS

A SEED DEVOTIONAL FOR WINNERS

DAILY DOSE

Purified, But Picking Out Your Own Poison

A SEED DEVOTIONAL FOR WINNERS

Good Morning Amazing People of GOD,

Bible Scriptures: 2nd Kings 5:21-22

A serious throwback moment: So picture me back in the day husky, two long ponytails, thick coke bottles glasses, and very short. My family lovingly calling me "Mikey", because I ate everything in sight and also did a little dance when it was really good. My favorite two spots my dad would take me to were Char-Hut and Carvel. We usually went to these places when he had a great day or when he did not have a great day. I tell this story because it started me on a journey of food being my friend and later my lover. It wasn't not my father's fault, because at any point I could have skipped the treat. However, I enjoyed picking my own delicious poison every time. I stepped up to the counter and ordered. Let's look at this in the text of the story of Gehazi; he willingly went back to the chariot, and lied and asked for "his poisons" which were the 2 talents of Sliver and two bags of clothing.

Question to ponder: Are you picking out and up your own poison? Take time to really think about it.

Have a thought provoking day and stay blessed.

A SEED DEVOTIONAL FOR WINNERS

A SEED DEVOTIONAL FOR WINNERS

DAILY DOSE

Purified, But Hiding

A SEED DEVOTIONAL FOR WINNERS

Good Morning Bold Believers in Christ,

Bible Scriptures: 2nd Kings 5:23-24 (NIV) "'By all means, take two talents,' said Naaman. He urged Gehazi to accept them, and then tied up the two talents of silver in two bags, with two sets of clothing. He gave them to two of his servants, and they carried them ahead of Gehazi. When Gehazi came to the hill, he took the things from the servants and put them away in the house. He sent the men away and they left."

So let's jump right in. Gehazi started off with a good intention, which became a selfish decision, then started running after trouble, and ultimately ended up picking out his own poison. Now we find him hiding his ill-gotten gifts and the walls are closing in fast.

Questions to ponder: What do you think Gerhazi is going to do? Have you ever felt like Gerhazi in this situation? If so when and what did you end up doing?

Have an awesome day.

A SEED DEVOTIONAL FOR WINNERS

A SEED DEVOTIONAL FOR WINNERS

DAILY DOSE

Purified, But The Question

A SEED DEVOTIONAL FOR WINNERS

Good Morning Cool and Creative Lovers of Christ, Bible Scriptures: 2nd Kings 5:25-27

The one question that got me in the most trouble with my mother growing up was, "Where have you been?" She usually would ask this question when she already knew the answer. I couldn't understand how she knew the answer when we didn't have cell phones back then. However, now I know that the HOLY Ghost kept her in the look. So in the text we see that Prophet Elisha has asked Gehazi where he has been, and even dropped a bombshell that his spirit was with him when he stopped the chariot. Elisha the prophet explained to Gehazi that this was not the time to seek rewards, but to change a man's life with the touch and word of the LORD with NO Strings attached. Yet, what became of Gehazi's poor decision making? He started out with a good intention, but ended up leaving with leprosy.

Please share what was one of the lessons you learned from Gehazi. Have a wonderful day.

A SEED DEVOTIONAL FOR WINNERS

A SEED DEVOTIONAL FOR WINNERS

DAILY DOSE

How Long Will You Wait

A SEED DEVOTIONAL FOR WINNERS

Good Morning Dazzling Doers of Christ,

Bible Scriptures: Joshua 18:1-6

How many times have you missed your promised land that GOD has given you? What excuses have you used? Have you talked yourself out of it? Did you let doubt and fear talk to you, assumed that too much time had passed you by, or were you too scared to fight for it. This week I would like to look at ways to Possess your promised land.

Key Seed 1: Know who you are and who's you are? Knowing who you are is accepting every part of you and loving YOURSELF unconditionally. Yet, knowing Who's you are is the Best because you are a wonderfully made Child of a Heavenly King, and don't you forget it. Please say the following Devine Decree aloud.

Devine Decree: I AM____and I am a wonderfully made child of the King of Kings and the Lord of Lords!!

Have a wonderful day.

A SEED DEVOTIONAL FOR WINNERS

A SEED DEVOTIONAL FOR WINNERS

DAILY DOSE

How Long Will You Wait?
Speak The Word

A SEED DEVOTIONAL FOR WINNERS

Good Morning Excellent Eagles in Christ,

Bible Scriptures: Joshua 18:1-6

What did God tell Moses to do to the mountain? Speak to it, or stay silent? The answer is to speak to it.

Key Seed 1: Speak the word! Today's word is very short, but powerful. In any and all situations speak the word that GOD spoke to you.

Question to ponder: Are you speaking to your mountains or are you staying mute?

Have a wonderful day.

A SEED DEVOTIONAL FOR WINNERS

A SEED DEVOTIONAL FOR WINNERS

DAILY DOSE

How Long Will You Wait? Know Your Rights

A SEED DEVOTIONAL FOR WINNERS

Good Morning Faithful 🔥 starters in the spirit, Bible Scriptures: Joshua 18:1-6

Key Seed 2: Know your Kingdom privileges and rights. Both the King and Queen have privileges and rights. They both have authority that demands respect, influence, an inheritance, knowledge, presence, and wisdom.

However, the KING has the ability to Decree an edict of death or life. So today take hold of your KINGLY privileges in your life and decree death to what is NOT serving you and speak life to what you want in your life.

Statement to ponder: List the things in your life that should be put to death.

Have a wonderful day.

Speak death to:	Speak life to:

A SEED DEVOTIONAL FOR WINNERS

A SEED DEVOTIONAL FOR WINNERS

DAILY DOSE

Know Your Heavenly Resources & Their Purpose

A SEED DEVOTIONAL FOR WINNERS

Good Morning GODLY Gifted Children, Bible Scriptures: Joshua 18:1-6

Key Seed: Know your heavenly resources and their purpose. Do you know your heavenly resources and what their purpose is? Many times we spend unneeded and unnecessary time trying to do things on our own when GOD has given us heavenly resources. Once you have discovered your heavenly resources ask GOD what their purpose is with you on that journey.

Have a wonderful day.

A SEED DEVOTIONAL FOR WINNERS

A SEED DEVOTIONAL FOR WINNERS

DAILY DOSE

Keeping GOD In The Center
Of Your Decision Making

A SEED DEVOTIONAL FOR WINNERS

Good Morning Heavenly Host Helpers, Topic: How long will you wait?

Bible Scriptures: Joshua 18:1-6

Imagine cooking rice on a stove that you assumed was on, and waiting 15 minutes for a finished product, only to discover that the stove was never turned on. This is what it looks like in the natural world when you don't consult God in your decisions.

Key Seed: Keeping GOD in the center of your decision making. In the story Joshua inquired of GOD.

Question to ponder: Do you keep GOD at the center of your decision making?

Have a wonderful day.

A SEED DEVOTIONAL FOR WINNERS

A SEED DEVOTIONAL FOR WINNERS

DAILY DOSE

Know That The LORD/GOD Never Fails

A SEED DEVOTIONAL FOR WINNERS

Good Morning Inspired People of GOD, Topic: How long will you wait?

Bible Scriptures: Joshua 21:43-45

Imagine you are a tightrope walker, and you are walking across a familiar high wire line, suddenly you have a misstep and at the last moment you feel as if you are going to fall head first, then you feel a hand carefully guiding you back and across the line to safety.

Key Seed: Know that the LORD/GOD never fails.

Just take a moment and look back over your life to a time, when things got rough and you were on the edge. Now, think about how GOD came to your rescue. Today share how GOD came through for you.

Have a wonderful day.

A SEED DEVOTIONAL FOR WINNERS

A SEED DEVOTIONAL FOR WINNERS

DAILY DOSE

Teaching & Telling About The Lessons Learned?

A SEED DEVOTIONAL FOR WINNERS

Good Morning Justified by Jesus lovers,

Topic: Do you remember the time?

Bible Scriptures: Joshua 24 (The chapter)

Opening Questions: When was the last time you remembered GOD's goodness in your life?

Take five seconds and close your eyes and think about GOD's goodness. Did you share it with someone? Did you share the whole story or just the parts that made you look good?

Today's Key Seed 1: Teaching and Telling about the lessons learned in the past. Today share your testimony in its entirety so others can get the most from it.

Have a wonderful day.

A SEED DEVOTIONAL FOR WINNERS

A SEED DEVOTIONAL FOR WINNERS

DAILY DOSE

Writing Down Those Wow Moments

A SEED DEVOTIONAL FOR WINNERS

Good Morning Kingdom Kids, Topic: Do you remember the time?

Bible Scriptures: Joshua 24 (The chapter)

Imagine being told about a promise 25 years ago and waiting for it to come to pass. Each year the agony of the wait seems to get heavier and heavier. Over time your faith may fluctuate, and at your most desperate points you try to fulfill the promise on your own, but fail. Yet when you give it over to God fully that is when your wow moment comes to pass.

Take a moment and think back to when GOD Wowed you!!!

Key Seed #2: Write Down those wow moments, and place them around you to keep your faith built up. For Example: GOD canceled my debt!!! GOD rescued me from an oppressive job.

Have a faith building day.

A SEED DEVOTIONAL FOR WINNERS

A SEED DEVOTIONAL FOR WINNERS

DAILY DOSE

Remember When You Cried Out To GOD

A SEED DEVOTIONAL FOR WINNERS

Good Morning Lovers of the LORD,

Topic: Do you remember the time?

Bible Scriptures: Joshua 24 (The chapter)

Think back to when you were a new parent, and how you responded to your child's cry. When you heard the cry, you were alert, quick to respond and filled the request with love. This is what it looks like when God responds to us when we are in trouble.

Key Seed 3: Remember when you cried out to GOD and how he responded to you.

****By looking at how GOD responded to you and your situation shows you his overwhelming concern and love for you.****

Have a wonderful day.

A SEED DEVOTIONAL FOR WINNERS

A SEED DEVOTIONAL FOR WINNERS

DAILY DOSE

Remember How GOD Pushed You Towards Your Destiny.

A SEED DEVOTIONAL FOR WINNERS

Good Morning Magnificent miracles from God, Topic: Do you remember the time?

Bible Scriptures: Joshua 24 (The chapter)

Remember when you first learned how to ride a bike, and you looked for your parents to guide you by the handlebars. The first time you failed, you wanted to give up, but they continued to encourage and push you to get back on the bike until you finally learned how to ride it.

Key Seed 4: Remember how GOD proclaimed, provided, protected, prospered, and pulled or pushed you towards your Destiny.

Think back to when you wanted to give up and GOD wouldn't let you.

Have a wonderful day.

A SEED DEVOTIONAL FOR WINNERS

A SEED DEVOTIONAL FOR WINNERS

DAILY DOSE

Remember How GOD Gave You Victories.

A SEED DEVOTIONAL FOR WINNERS

Good Morning Natural Beauties formed by GOD, Topic: Do you remember the time?

Bible Scriptures: Joshua 24 (The chapter)

Key Seed 5: Remember how GOD gave you the victories in the face of your enemies.

Even when they cursed you he still blessed you PS: That was your praise break

Have a wonderful day.

A SEED DEVOTIONAL FOR WINNERS

A SEED DEVOTIONAL FOR WINNERS

DAILY DOSE

What Is A Blessing?

A SEED DEVOTIONAL FOR WINNERS

Good Morning Outstanding and Obedient Children of God, Topic: The Blessing pt.1 (What is a blessing?)

A blessing is a Barak which is Hebrew for praise, congratulate, and/or salute. Another Hebrew word is esher which means one's happiness. So when GOD blesses you he is honoring you with his gift of happiness. For example, when GOD blessed Hanna with Samuel. Or when GOD took the Children of Israel out from under the oppressive grasp of Pharaoh. Today share how GOD has blessed you.

Have an outstanding day.

A SEED DEVOTIONAL FOR WINNERS

A SEED DEVOTIONAL FOR WINNERS

DAILY DOSE

What Does The Blessing Mean?

A SEED DEVOTIONAL FOR WINNERS

Good Morning Powerful People of Christ, Topic: The Blessing pt2

Key Seed 2: What does the Blessing means?

Imagine being at a wedding and the ring bearer comes down the aisles shouting "Here comes the bride, Here comes the bride"... this statement is a declaration that the bride has been choosen and favored by the groom to be his wife. This is what it looks like in the spirit when God provides you with a blessing.

1. A public declaration of being favored with and by GOD.

2. Having the power to prosper and have a life of success.

***Remember that everyday GOD is setting you up for a life filled with blessings. ***

Enjoy your day.

A SEED DEVOTIONAL FOR WINNERS

A SEED DEVOTIONAL FOR WINNERS

DAILY DOSE

The Posture

A SEED DEVOTIONAL FOR WINNERS

Good Morning Children of On-time GOD, Topic: The Blessing (The Posture)

Do you know the posture of a blessing? It is kneeling, because you are in a place to receive. Today in your quiet time get in the Powerful posture of receiving the many blessings GOD has for you.

Have a spirit led day.

A SEED DEVOTIONAL FOR WINNERS

A SEED DEVOTIONAL FOR WINNERS

DAILY DOSE

What Can Bless You?

A SEED DEVOTIONAL FOR WINNERS

Good Morning Quiet time faith builders,

Topic: The Blessing (Who can bless you?)

In the Bible there are many examples of people blessing others. For example, GOD blessing the animals (Gen 1:22); GOD blessing Adam and Eve (Gen 1:28); Abraham being blessed for his obedience (Gen 22:16-18) and Isaac and Rebekah (Gen 24). So who can be blessed? Anyone with a covenant relationship with GOD, Jesus, and the Holy Spirit. Today step boldly into the blessings that you have with all the authority, dominion, and power that GOD has gifted you with.

Have a spectacular day.

A SEED DEVOTIONAL FOR WINNERS

A SEED DEVOTIONAL FOR WINNERS

DAILY DOSE

The Blessing:
The Different Types Of Blessings

A SEED DEVOTIONAL FOR WINNERS

Good Morning Radically Rescued Children of GOD,

Topic: The Blessing (The different types of blessings.)

There are many types of blessings. However, we are going to focus on the Ceremonial Blessing. This one blessing is broken up into three parts. The 1st one is the family blessing, where someone in the family can bless you or you blessing them. Such as when Jacob blesses his sons (Gen 49). The second one is the governmental blessing. This is where someone in a high position blessed you. For example, when King David blessed Abigail (1 Sam 25) and later married her. The third one is the priestly blessing. This is where someone in the spiritual realm blesses you. As in the case where Melchizedek blessed Abraham. (Heb. 7). Today take the time to bless someone.

Have a wonderful day.

A SEED DEVOTIONAL FOR WINNERS

A SEED DEVOTIONAL FOR WINNERS

DAILY DOSE

The Blessing Pt. 2

A SEED DEVOTIONAL FOR WINNERS

Good Morning Seed Sowers of GOD's Goodness and Glory,

Topic: The Blessing pt. 3

Bible Scriptures: Ephesians 1:4

Think back to when you were in Elementary School at PE or recess getting ready to play kickball. The coach would pick two students to be the captains of the teams and to pick the rest of the team. So picture me short, fat, two long ponytails and thick coke bottle glasses. Most of the time I was never chosen for a team, sometimes it hurt and other times not at all. So one Saturday while talking to "my angel," my grandmother, it came up. Her words to me were that YOU HAVE BEEN CHOSEN BY GOD. She would say whenever you feel lonely know that GOD has chosen you. So I just wanted to share this with someone this morning: know that you HAVE BEEN CHOSEN BY GOD.

Devine Decree: Stop and say this aloud: I have been chosen by GOD!!!

Have a wonderful day

A SEED DEVOTIONAL FOR WINNERS

A SEED DEVOTIONAL FOR WINNERS

DAILY DOSE

Predestined For GOD's Goodness & Greatness

A SEED DEVOTIONAL FOR WINNERS

Good Morning Talented Teachers of GOD's word, Topic: The Blessing pt. 4

Bible Scriptures: Ephesians 1:5

Today's word is short but powerful!!! Think about this: You were on GOD's heart, mind, and mouth before you were a thought in your mother's mind and a seed in your father's trousers.

Remember that You were predestined for GOD's goodness and his greatness.*

Devine Decree: Say this aloud: I am predestined for GOD's goodness and I am destined for greatness!!!

Have a wonderful day.

A SEED DEVOTIONAL FOR WINNERS

A SEED DEVOTIONAL FOR WINNERS

DAILY DOSE

Your Praise Is A Part Of Your Warfare

A SEED DEVOTIONAL FOR WINNERS

Good Morning Ultimately Unique Children of GOD, Topic: The Blessing pt. 5

Bible Scriptures: Ephesians 1:6

One of my favorite memories of my grandmother's home is her humming and singing hymns while cooking. She would hum and sing hymns throughout the house all day. As I got older, I realized that she was fighting spiritual warfare in a different way. She taught us many things, in addition to teaching my sister and I how to fight spiritually.

Put a praise on your life!! Today put your mighty praise on your day.

Remember your praise is a part of your warfare.

Have a powerfully praise filled day.

A SEED DEVOTIONAL FOR WINNERS

A SEED DEVOTIONAL FOR WINNERS

DAILY DOSE

Forgiven And Redeemed

A SEED DEVOTIONAL FOR WINNERS

Good Morning Victorious Children of GOD,

Topic: The Blessing pt. 6

Bible Scriptures: Ephesians 1:7

Catch this: you have been forgiven and redeemed by the Savior. Take a moment to remember and share how GOD rescued you from the hands of the enemy and has freely forgiven for you.

Devine Decree: Say this aloud: I have been forgiven and redeemed by the King of Kings.

Have a wonderful day.

A SEED DEVOTIONAL FOR WINNERS

A SEED DEVOTIONAL FOR WINNERS

DAILY DOSE

Extra Dose Of His Wisdom

A SEED DEVOTIONAL FOR WINNERS

Good Morning World Wide Winners in Christ, Topic: The Blessing pt. 7

Bible Scriptures: Ephesians 1:8

Imagine this, Jesus Christ wants us to be wrapped up warmly in his wisdom and understanding. Every day he seeks to give you more of it so you can handle what is coming ahead. Today ask Jesus to give you an extra dose of his wisdom and understanding.

Have a wonderful day.

A SEED DEVOTIONAL FOR WINNERS

A SEED DEVOTIONAL FOR WINNERS

DAILY DOSE

What Does Praise Do?

A SEED DEVOTIONAL FOR WINNERS

Good Morning EXCELLENT Children of GOD, Topic: Praise (What does praise do?)

Bible Scriptures: PSALM 147:1 (NIV) "Praise the Lord. How good it is to sing praises to our God, how pleasant and fitting to praise him!"

Think back to your childhood. Remember the student who always complemented or praised the teacher. They were doing two things: building the teacher up and getting the teacher's attention, which may have had great results if the student was struggling in any subject. So let's look at this in the spiritual realm.

Every time you open your mouth and heart and give the LORD your praise. It builds him up, brings pleasure to him, and gets his attention. Today use your body, heart, mind, and mouth and get your praise on!!!

Have a praise filled day.

A SEED DEVOTIONAL FOR WINNERS

A SEED DEVOTIONAL FOR WINNERS

DAILY DOSE

Praise

A SEED DEVOTIONAL FOR WINNERS

Good Morning Youthful Leaders in Christ, Topic: Praise

Bible Scriptures: Revelation 7:12 (NIV)

"saying: 'Amen! Praise and glory and wisdom and thanks and honor and power and strength be to our God for ever and ever Amen!'

Your praise is a daily faith builder.

Divine Decree: Say this aloud: My name is___, and I am a mighty praiser. Every time I open my heart, mind, mouth, and spirit to the LORD. I build up my confidence, connection, and faith.

Have a faith building day.

A SEED DEVOTIONAL FOR WINNERS

Tune Into: The Seed Sowing Sistah Movement Radio Show

Contact Us: for Sponsorship or Advertising Opportunities

Book Patrice: for Keynote Speaking and Trainings
Email Inquiries: seedsowingsistahmovement@gmail.com

About The Author

Patrice is a happily retired educator, author, consultant, licensed mental health counselor, entrepreneur, and community leader who utilizes her life experiences to help people of all ages reach their full potential. As a seasoned educator, Patrice taught in the Broward and Miami-Dade County Public School systems for a combined total of 16 years. For several years, she served as a volunteer with the I AM Ministries of Miami-Dade and Broward County working with teen girls co-facilitating the "Divas Destined for Greatness" groups.

In addition, she also co-facilitated a weekly women's group called "The Women's Empowerment Hour." In 2011, she was awarded "The Woman of Empowerment Award."

Patrice's motto is simple yet powerful: "Be inspired to be yourself, Be inspired to empower someone else." These words not only describe her life, they will one day be the legacy and the message that she leaves behind with the global community.

Patrice inspires the millions on a weekly basis with her world-renowned Radio show The Seed Sowing Sistah Movement.

www.ingramcontent.com/pod-product-compliance
Lightning Source LLC
Chambersburg PA
CBHW031148160426
43193CB00008B/290